Three Hundred Poems

Komi Olafimihan

Write Bloody North

writebloodynorth.ca

Copyright © Komi Olafimihan, 2023.

All rights reserved. No part of this book may be used, performed, or reproduced in any manner whatsoever without written permission from the publisher except in the case of brief quotations embodied in critical articles or reviews.

First edition.
ISBN: 978-1-7781626-0-2

Cover Design by Maria Kassab
Interior Layout by Winona León
Edited by Tawhida Tanya Evanson
Copyedited by Stuart Ross

Type set in Bergamo.

Write Bloody North
Toronto, ON

Support Independent Presses
writebloodynorth.ca

This book was generously funded by

*To my wife Donisha Prendergast,
whose love and patience has been a source of deep encouragement.*

THREE HUNDRED POEMS

Three Hundred Poems

Introduction 13

Chapter 1

The Lady in the House 17
Roses in the Car 18
Ebenezer 19
Afrofuturistic Museum 20
Slavery Post 21
The Black Vote 22
To Love an Island 23
Walk on Water 24
Blue Burn 25
Five Teshi 26
The Call 27

Chapter 2

Kiss 31
Protection 32
Prune 33
Fatherhood 34
Tears 35
Rebel 36
Wings 37
Write 38
Anchor 39
Three I's 40
Desire 41
Inspection 42
No Commitment 43
A Glimpse through the Curtain 44

Chapter 3

Common Ground 49
Wedding Poem 50
The One 51
Life 52
Strange Times 53
Running on the Beach 54
False Alarm 55
Across the Border 56
Germination 57
Soul Ties 58
Crown 59
Eructation 60
Oya 61
Koboko 62
Godfather 63
Thieves 64
Burning Finger 65
Narrow Escape 66
Small TV 68
Tank 69
Black Foam 70
Broken Stencil 71

Chapter 4

The Slap 75
The Vision 76
Common Room Survival 77
Packo Flakes 78
Boarding-House Currency 79
Reminders 80
Betrayal 81
The Space Between Us 82
Bleeding Towel 85
Imprisoned 86
The Legend of Don Shaver 87
Redemption 88
Habesha 89
Cosmic Rain 90
Solution 91

Black Bodies	92
Crossover	94
1968	95
Sankofa	97
About the Author	101

Introduction

I have always been intrigued by the Biblical story of the Jewish prophet Gideon—the warrior who led an army of three hundred soldiers to victory over the Midianites in the book of Judges. Growing up in a Christian household, I was privy to discussions about Biblical stories and their meanings and translations. Gideon is remembered as a man of faith; he sought God when the children of Israel had turned their backs and worshipped idols, and his call was answered.

When crafting this book, I drew inspiration from the story of how he was led by God to select his army of three hundred soldiers. When the people of Midian and Amalek had crossed the Jordan River, Gideon amassed an army to fight them. The number of men gathered was well over thirty thousand, and Gideon received word that the number was too high. If the Israelite army prevailed over the Midianites, they would have no cause to believe it was the Lord who had granted them the victory. He told all those who were afraid that they should return home, and when they had left, the number had reduced to ten thousand. But the number was still too large, so he instructed the men to go to the river and drink. Some of them knelt down and cupped the water in their hands, while others put their faces to the river and lapped like dogs. Those who lapped the water were three hundred—and those were the soldiers he chose to form the army.

At the start of COVID-19, I began writing poetry prompted by the titles and stories of the books on my bookshelf. At the time, no one knew how long the lockdowns would last and how disruptive they would be. Welcoming the birth of my son, I was inspired to write poems about my life experiences, lessons I have learned along the way, and some I wish I had read in a book. This volume is a collection of the metaphorical three hundred lessons I chose to represent some of my thoughts and views, hoping to paint a better picture of who I am, for the world to know and my son to one day better understand.

CHAPTER 1

The Lady in the House

This is for the lady in the house
cultivator of all things bright and beautiful.

I sing it for the lady in the house.
With her back turned
her eyes focussed far away on the contents of her hands.
She is content.

She is in full control of the circumstances of her life.

She who will one day bring forth life
cuts through an onion
dices up old memories of promises unkept.
Something about onions makes her cry.
Science suggests sulfenic acid, a chemical irritant
but she knows it's because there are never multiple layers to the truth.
The truth is wholesome
cut and dried.

This is for the lady in the house
the one holding the disco ball
in the centre of her belly.

She pours colourful spices and black pepper
into a non-stick black pot.
Palm oil and water mix
making the house smell like Africa.
She is content.
She is the continent
cut and dried.

This is for the lady in the house
cultivator of all things bright and beautiful.

Roses in the Car

By the rivers of Babylon I sat down
and wept unbearably for my unborn child.
No pronoun to refer to your spirit
just a ball of white light on a black screen.
I carried a bouquet of twelve white roses
but let them wither in the back seat of the car.
Shaved my head bald
and saw disappointment dagger friends' faces.
I still wonder what they know
who saw the light extinguished in the pupils of our eyes.

Ebenezer

Invisible Man,
never managed to read the book.
Instead, imagined its existence
on the bookshelf would somehow
make the story visible to me.
Given to me by a twin
who I would later tell to get lost
when they questioned
my eternal love for my love.

I was once a faceless man.
Washed my face clean with a black cloth
after dancing with three mermaids
covered in white dots and African prints.
They were sirens luring me to drink the Kool-Aid,
confirmation that African juju travels across the water.

So I buried my seed in the soft soil of my trauma
and joined a tribe of brownskin Indians.
Israel embraced me and Pakistan opened its heart.
A fruitful tree grew from the earth,
and we will mark this place
and call it "Ebenezer."

Afrofuturistic Museum

Culture and Imperialism go together like
heritage museums and Indigenous blood
or the Impressionist paintings
of Monet, Manet, Gaugin.
All those solarized nudes
lustful imperialists called "impious."

Money still green in a land where
crooked cops shoot gene-carrying
blue-jeaned Black boys in their homes
with taser guns or bullets that burn like lasers
for target practice.

The CPP cock crows in Benin
awakening the black spots on a cheetah
the broad stripes of a zebra, and a giraffe
sneaking its long neck in
through the side door.

In Accra
Kwame Nkrumah
still polishes the Black Star
pointing one finger to the heavens.
Thousands thronged
in the midst of motorbikes and rainstorms
under the sky at Jamestown.

We heard
there was a culture of xenophobia
unfortunately, eating at the bones of some of those
liberated by Mandela Madiba Nelson
on the soil where Zulu warriors
once strategized and overcame their true invaders.
Imagine—
and the self-righteous once pointed fingers
at Winnie, condemning her.
Per capita income the consequences of thieves' actions.
Dissatisfaction is a ticking time bomb
and the recipe for peace is education.
Symbiotic cohabitation.
Something called sharing.

SLAVERY POST

Some Freed African-Americans
owned slaves of their own.

Some Free Africans
own slaves of their own.

Some slaves currently make long-distance calls
on borrowed phones behind fences in detention camps
to some women in the diaspora
who are raising
funds to help them
buy back their freedom.

Some will hear and ignore
some will hear and heed
till slavemassas be no more
and all slaves be freed.

The Black Vote

Who said we are all the same?

We are all the same
however

Ethnicity is as real as
the northern vote
the western vote
the eastern vote
the south-south vote

the coat of arms looks like
three elephants leaning on a shield
with a ribbon reading
"Inclusivity is the teardrop of the Megastate"

To Love an Island

The goat is grazing
chewing the cud.
We cut palm trees out of cardboard boxes
and used the recycled stencil to time travel.

Now, we both have given
a piece of our hearts to an island
that may never recognize us as equals.

The last time
we arrived from the motherland
they picked us up
fed us home-cooked food from the horn
in a kitchen smaller than the human eye.
As if they knew
the purple blood in our hearts
had been turned indigo by camel toe
like tie and dye
drying on the roof
of a building decaying
in a deserted dystopian city.

Walk on Water

It is time to walk on water
to stop doubting and step out in faith
to know that the one who called
is out there on a boat and will catch you
if you doubt again on the way.

It is clear that you fear
you may sink to the bottom
if you do not paddle.

But you are both the top and the bottom
so walk on the water
let the soles of your feet
meet the cold touch of liquid.

Catch your balance, take a deep breath
and focus on the call
the vibration of voice
swishing your heart.

Blue Burn

Interesting to know
that invisible organisms
can cause deadly diseases, eh?

Before we talk about political hygiene
we must first master personal hygiene, on a spiritual level:
There can be no talk of freedom or emancipation
as long as the dishes are piled up in the sink
and garbage stinks up the kitchen.

Let us reintroduce the blue bin.
Blue for Sudan
bin for the Janjaweed.
Green is the colour of our true love's hair.
Blue-green is this jewelled planet.

Five Teshi

In primary school, Mr. Anyanwu
was my first art teacher.
Class five Teshi named after
what I thought was a river
in opposition to class five Mariga.

He was a short man
with skin the colour of mahogany.
An Igbo man, as proud and productive as the chalk in his hand.
He didn't write notes on the board
he scratched life drawings of buckets and brooms
arranged like models on the classroom floor.

Flawless, finessed, with style.
When the bell rang
he would sometimes leave the drawing on the board
until the next day.
I would stare at it in the classroom
till my mother came to pick me up
sit me up in the car and drive me home.

The next day before general assembly
the drawing would have vanished from the board
and Mr. Anyanwu would be there teaching
what I would later come to understand as
"further mathematics."
The proven hunches—angles and curves—
that make a household profit.

The Call

Alpha of Omega
the beginning of the end of the story
through cosmic osmosis
like the aligning of energy.

A red ribbon tied the spirits back together
after breaking open the seal.
The curtain was ripped down the middle and
three musicians shared one trumpet
blew air like a whirlwind into the sails
of a once-abandoned ship.

The instrument lies still in a black box
while there is talk of nuclear and biological warfare.
Global warming, food shortage, world hunger and thirst
and plague after plague after plague
as if the end of the world has not already come
for some.
Long before Black Panther and Wakanda.

Ask those who were awoken by shadows
in the middle of night, guns drawn
and sounding like trumpets.

CHAPTER 2

Kiss

I was thirteen and her skin was ebony black
beyond a doubt the smartest girl in the class.
I walked with her from her classroom to mine—
my wingmen had helped to ensure the environment was dark.
We had planned it for a week and today was the day.
I didn't have dinner that night
respectfully refused the beans and fried plantain the prefect served
saving the fresh mint of my breath.

When I met her outside her classroom door
she looked at me through her glasses
and slipped her fingers into mine.
We walked down the stairs that seemed to take forever
past the rose bushes, the library and the computer lab.
When we arrived at my classroom
we closed the door
and shut our eyes.
No lesson ever tasted so sweet.

Protection

It shocked the neighbourhood
but I had seen how popular
he was with the ladies.
Witnessed him convince a groundnut seller
or two to follow him to the quarters
on quite a few occasions.

When he passed away
people spoke in hushed voices
as if he could hear them from beyond the grave.

Before then I thought "condom" was a powder
men drank to get strong.

Prune

Harvest the seed
plant the seed to harvest
there must be digging and plowing and sweating
water and air and sunshine
there must be conversation and pruning
plants talk a lot
so much so you may have to beg them
to shut up every once in a while
pruning their beseeching.

Fatherhood

What is the full measure of a man?
I have seen sisterhood first-hand
and my life is testament to brotherhood.
But the intricacies of how my father produced a perfect record
one without blemish or blame
eludes me.

So I start where he started
with commitment and vision
a single room and a mattress
a head full of stories
and my heart safe in the eyes of my love.
She lies in the gazebo, calm
watching over the baby soon to be born
after a few full moons shine their light on our changing bodies.

Speedboats race across the water in Montego Bay
while strangers converse with the wind.

I say a prayer of gratitude for our baby
girl or boy

awaiting the birth of a messiah's parents.

Tears

When grieving
tears, like soap
wash away unfinished conversations
unresolved issues with the one now floating in the cosmos
with supernatural beings we call spirits.

Who knew our tear ducts could touch our conscience
with soft fingers
cuddle with care our sobbing hearts.

But Jesus wept.

Rebel

Rebellions are rarely successful
and when they are
they leave a vacuum
where greed and corruption fester.

Therefore: internal revolution
before external rebellion.

Wings

Meditating on the life of Professor Pius Adesanmi
or the little I got to experience of him.
What I take away from his life is
do well, do good and be consistent.
He believed in God, it was evident from his last online post.
I wish I had known him earlier, during my university days.

Some meditations scare me
not in the sense of horror but implication.
I set my eyes toward Ile-Ife with a yearning for enlightenment.

In sight and in might I will praise him: That's my piety.
Bishop Desmond Tutu said
"God is not a Christian."
Indeed, "religion" ain't got a prayer
in any contest with faith.

Write

I tell you
there is a perfect place to write.
Where?
Right beside the centre
for innovation
where poison ivy
grows on the aluminum fence
blocking off the collapsing buildings of ideas
with caved-in roofs
the brick and stone walls exposed
like a nipple.

The ripple effects of decadent thoughts
actions, habits and character.
Simple.

Two puffs of smoke and an Audi rolled in
with red leather seats and music blasting through speakers
integrated into butterfly doors.

Please note the
"No Parking" sign
wear your mask
wash your hands
and recognize that this is the perfect place
to write up
rights
so abrupt
is the corruption.

Anchor

The man beside me at church
wiped his hands on his shirt after shaking my hand.
I wondered what it meant
considered racism, germophobia, the fear of the looming plague.

I stopped smoking the herb.
Its chemicals are evidently not good for my system
but the truth is
I've been smoking the herb
since the herb was smoked.
Back when they called her S.K. Sasha
Loud the delightful.

There are no more coincidences in my life.
All things have come full circle
since I hit rock bottom in an emergency room
like a rusty anchor
stabilizing a rocking ship.
There was no one to hold my hand
nor any ganja to send up smoke signals.

Three I's

Dear Angel,
there are things you should know about me.
Things that constantly wander in my mind.
Like, what do I do with all I have seen
all the testimonies I have witnessed?
Where do I store the lessons
the look of judgment in the eyes of strangers
that has shown me my nakedness?

I wonder
if I am capable of handling what I have asked for
what I have been blessed with.

It feels like one drop of the right thing opened my eyes
and the third eye will never shut.
I have the thousand-yard stare.

Desire

It felt good
to write
to release
to let thoughts flow out of pen
like they do in my head.
To breathe
to stretch out an idea
like a stream of consciousness.
To wonder
to refuse to bow
to be a slave
to one's desires.

Inspection

I feel responsible
sometimes irresponsible
for joining our legacies together.
It was not premeditated
not pre-calculated—
instinctive
I guess.
I will no longer
blame the boarding-house bully
who ordered me to draw pornographic illustrations of things I didn't know
to be on the lookout while he smoked cigarettes
behind the showers
who forced me to go hungry for his entertainment
told us it didn't matter
laughed in our faces and spat in our eyes.

I heard a boy strangled a boy
for wetting the bed
but the boy didn't die.
So he took him back and did it again.
He was kicked out of school
and now he wanders.

The baby was God
pulled out with a hanger
for fear of what her parents would say.

No Commitment

No commitment
is what makes a cactus die beside a jar full of water
what keeps the bills unpaid, bed unlaid
milk and vegetables still at the grocery store.
Sometimes
no commitment looks lost from across the street.
It makes us want to hug it, save it
take it to the moon and back.
But it takes commitment to get there.
It takes commitment to build a rocket ship.
No commitment will leave you
with a bolt, spanner and maybe a few nuts
committed to your failure.

A Glimpse through the Curtain

This one's for the keepers of books
the ones who relish the sight and smell of a physical copy.

These are my confessions
you may call it the actual book and revelation.
The truth is my thesis.
Improvisation in architecture appears
to be proof that God is indeed real.

I have pondered the consequences of my actions
if I open my mouth and talk.
To actually speak my testimony

felt like a battle
as if steel swords were drawn in the spiritual realm
and opposing armies clashed in the
art studio I had rented to complete a commission.
It was as if I had caught a glimpse of the face of the divine
while trying to construct it from a description.
I heard myself speak in a language I did not understand
felt my eyes roll and my hand scribble verses once memorized
onto the white walls in red and black ink for all to see.
There was no space between reality and fiction
the large painting had moved from wall to floor in my absence.
I was one with my assignment.

Chapter 3

COMMON GROUND

It appears to some in the diaspora
that to build Africa into
what It could be
we need to say yes to change
change from within.
And say no to the things
that hinder growth
and lay focus on the places
where ideas can bloom and flourish.
To invest in the potential of our youth
and remember the innate powers
of our ancestors streaming through our veins.

Wedding Poem

I guess it's time to make it official
whatever that means.
You and I both know we have been
Paddington Bear and Thomas the Tank Engine.
It is a special occasion
in the midst of chaos and school exams.
We have carved our love in the snow.
My love for you is quite
radical.

Like when you wear your hat backwards
and I have to sit there and think about the future
of the tiny house movement.
You are quite
radical.
Imagine
we travelled to the village to cook
bush tea for my grandma.
Are you mad?
I love you.
So radical.
This was supposed to be a signing ceremony.
Now we have stepped into the garden and opened a paradox box.
We are manifesting our love in stages.
For ages I will remember the first time
you smiled at me and instantly saw through my heart.
As we take our vows
know I will love and support you for as long as I shall live.
For as long as we shall live
we will live to declare the works of the creator in the land of the living.
Selah.

The One

You are the egg
the one you've been waiting for
the person you expected to appear in the sky
dressed in beautiful gold and black
orange and white
the one to pollinate your flowers
excite your imagination
whisper in your ears
voyage you across foreign lands and salty seas.

You are the change
trapped in your cocoon
incubating.
Going through a midlife crisis
breaking your beak
making it sharper
scratching your talons against solid rock
pulling out your feathers.
Don't matter none:
Your wings are being born.

Life

The day I found out I was having a boy
I sat in a sushi restaurant in the market
overlooking the café Barack Obama visited
when he came to Ottawa.
The nurse's voice on the other end of the line
sounded just as excited as I was.
As if she knew the news would come
as a surprise to everyone who knew.
I recorded the call to remember the joy.
The tongue is a powerful tool
capable of painting life
and prophesying death
unless the heart is doing the talking.

Strange Times

As we were saying
it is definitely time to be great again
to look through the cloud of the virus
the smokescreen
exposing the inadequacy of our leaders to respond pragmatically
to avoid the deadly cough.
We are witnessing
the new norms
turning the wheels of the paradigm shift
masquerading airborne pollutants threatening human survival.
The platform of social aid has begun to descend
from the federal, provincial and local government kitchens
and the majority are on level 333.

The first 33 cases came from Wuhan, China
and journalists, keepers of the truth
were forced to keep quiet while others went missing
their mothers pleading and crying
on YouTube channels.

As we were saying
it is definitely time to be great again
to acknowledge the courage of the doctors
the nurses, the receptionists
who, out of the kindness of their hearts, the expanse of their expertise
the almost militant dedication to ensuring we are safe and healthy
expose themselves daily
to the arrows of death.

Running on the Beach

These are the poems that made it through the weekend
visited repressed memories in my sleep
forced me to sit down in front of my easel and reach for the pen
sat on pages like her royal highness on a pedestal
with a foundation somewhere deep in the Atlantic Ocean
where screams from the ancestors
still echo like rocket engines
counted as the blazing sun sets
to set fire to the horizon.

False Alarm

I lost my cigarettes today
and have decided not to find them.

ACROSS THE BORDER
In memory of George Floyd

Just across the border
when we were huddled in with our loved ones
noses and mouths covered with blue masks
waiting for the pandemic to end.
Waiting in long lines for limited food supply
at the grocery store.
Hysterically banging our pots and pans in unison
at 7:30 every evening
in support of the essential workers
returning home from the frontlines.

From the frontlines
there are tales of looters
camouflaged in the crowd of protesters
breaking windows of department stores
stealing gold, sneakers
and burning down the fabric of society
unleashing the repressed anger of the people
on the people.

His blood cries out from the concrete.
I buried three cowries in his honour
and hope his life will never be overshadowed.
committed in broad daylight

Germination

Flowers are beginning to grow from our faces
they were watered by salty tears
shed on skin still tender from being indoors too long

Soul Ties

Soul ties
made by gazing transfixed
at the left eye of a lover.
The translucent scars
accumulating on an iris
become as real as
strawberry milkshake or
chocolate pudding pie
forsaking memories we wish we had never had.
Whose words carved us into ice sculptures
with red beating hearts
pumping blood into our spirits
reminding us of who
we constantly think we are.

CROWN

Today we became a family.
My wife, my son and I.
Three beings.
Right there, in the hospital room
With the doctor, small but mighty
the midwives catering to every contraction
checking every pulse.

Your pulse maintained a rhythm
creating a royal purple hue
enveloping the room with hope.

And then we saw the crown of your head.
The crown on your head is real.

Eructation

Grandma left today.
Now, it is just Mommy, Daddy and little baby
don't know how we will manage.
The first night you came home
I watched you sleep beside your mother in a cot.
Both of you had your arms stretched over your heads
and when you moved, she moved
synchronized
like the umbilical cord was still attached.
I could see it in my mind's eye
glowing with love
as real as the look on your face
right before you release
all the excess air.

Oya

Balance
confusion break bone
Multiplicity and entanglements
will lead to sadness in old age
balance.

According to the fisherman
the options of fish in the sea are boundless
so transplant yourself from the pond
and choose one.

Balance
confusion break bone
you may feel trapped in the cabin
but remember the door is always open
the sun is shining
and the elements are alive.

Oya.
Balance.

Koboko

Alkebulan
sounds a little bit strange
if you haven't heard the name before.

Al- like AlHajji, aluminium foil, Almanjari, Al Sharpton's sharp tongue, Alta Vista.
Ke- like AK-17, K.D., K, sugarcane, koboko cane.
Bu- like honey boo, Boo the bear, Boo reaching for black matter, boo like Casper.
Lan- time for Europe to trigger all the landmines left behind in the Congo.

Godfather

Dr. Samaila is my godfather—
he made many young men feel special
as if they were indeed his sons.
Through him I learned of places like
Zangon Kataf and Zazzau
not through history books now banned from the Nigerian curriculum.
You may call it a manifestation of oral tradition.
When I dream about Kaduna and artistic concepts for KD 004
an attempt to mark time differently through the documentation of
catastrophic social issues.
I think about the afternoon he took us to Malali Market
to get measured for our first kaftans.
He made many young men feel special
like we belonged in a rainbow tribe
from various parts of a fragmented country.

Thieves

The realization
the poems are burning
like Molotov cocktails in the hands of a child soldier
awoken from a deep sleep the cold night
he saw the robber struck down with
a bow and arrow.

Close to the man who kept bloodhounds and
rare breeds of dogs known to tear a man to pieces.

We were raised to guard our yards against thieves
who pulled out the robust air conditioner
and crept in through the square opening in the wall.

Better to set broken glass in the vacancy
and sweat
than to weep for loss.

Burning Finger

The finger
floated over the golden plate and pointed
toward the sleeping boy.
He thought it was a dream.
A witch camouflaged as a nanny
had been spotted high up in the trees.
We burned the garri and groundnut she left as bait
but the paraphernalia did not burn.
Exu.

Narrow Escape

We smoked shisha and disappeared
into the night.
Reminisced about old days
and potential business opportunities
like we had actually been friends before.
We both knew that deep down
we shared the same pain of loss.

We arrived at your parents' in a taxi cab
with dreams of discovering more about our bodies.
Thick sultry terracotta lips
covered in lipstick red like crimson sky
asked me to wait in the abandoned building down the road
while the gate to your house remained closed.

When my phone died
tired of waiting and thinking
realizing I was indeed alone
I decided to find my way home
walk the dusty red clay road through
suburbia back to the highway
and hitchhike to Abuja.

With sweat dripping down my face
and my clothes covered in dust
I surprised three dubious men burying a secret
in the middle of the night, talking in hushed voices
in a language I knew but couldn't understand.

It could have been a body.
It could have been a cow.

I ran in any direction my feet would carry me
afraid to shout and draw attention
lost in a maze of buildings and roads
that all looked alike to a son of the soil
who had been away for far too long.

When I got back to the safety of my hotel
a search party had been assembled
to comb the streets and look for me
a foreigner who had wandered too deep
into the outskirts of the city.

Small TV

Have you ever been surprised by tears
escaping through the corners of your eyes?
Felt the wet warmth of fresh salt water
cascade down the landscape of your face?

Have you heard the soft cry of a newborn baby
knowing anguish has been screamed out
by a warrior of a mother
after long years of suffering?

Have you heard the whimper of a puppy
under a dusty old car or the quiet whisper of a family
taking refuge in the guestroom because armed robbers
are stealing the big TV?

We watched the Twin Towers
come down on the small TV
my father placed on the now-empty big TV stand.
His hands, bandaged from the wounds left behind
after a cutlass came down like lightning
when he opened his bedroom door.

Did you shed tears while watching the smoke cover the screens
and the bodies leap from the towers
or are you preoccupied with the conspiracy theories
about who showed up to work that day and who didn't?

Will you shed tears for my father's sabred hands
our big TV lost to a conspiracy of thugs?

Well, yes, weep.
But the faithful know
the world is a conspiracy of tears.

Tank

While we were proud
for climbing to the apex
of the water tank with girls we loved
the real ones walked through the bush
in the middle of the night to the nearby town
through disputed land
with torch lights and crumpled notes
through grassland and tall trees
where ancestral beings talked
to boarding-house children
huddled together against a common cause.

When they came back
they had treasures from the city
and tales of adventure while
crossing the fence of the school
both to and from the land of sweet potato and Gidigbo.
After lights out
we watched them sneak out
under the cover of night
while the snoring of the guards
could be heard
along the corridor.

Dressed in black with empty bags to bring back spoils
and scavenged fruits from the forest.
The fence was cut with pliers
and they took turns crawling through the sharp opening
watching for dangerous animals and plants.
The barking of wild dogs
could be heard in the distance
but the hope of getting to and back
from the city before the break of dawn
spawned young men out of boys
whose testicles had yet to descend.

Black Foam

The first time I moved out
I took the couch from the family basement
carefully placed it deep in the moving truck
before the boxes of books, suitcases of clothes
and artistic paraphernalia.

Drove to my comrade's abode
honked twice and loaded up his belongings.
When we arrived in the big apple of a city
we placed our boxes around the hardwood floor like
red bricks and mortar.

We lifted the stolen couch up the L-shaped steps
encouraging each other along the way:
"Well done, man!"
"Hey! Watch your elbow!"
The couch would not fit through the door.

We put it back in the moving truck and ate lunch—
spicy vegetarian biryani and Afghan chicken
with a Sprite to wash it down—
spoke about dreams and the possibility
of obtaining some plants
from a man who had travelled in from Saskatoon.

Before the sun went down
we took the couch to a recycling plant
watched it roll down the conveyor belt
poured libations and said a short prayer.
On the long drive back home
we stopped at a furniture store and
got a futon instead:
"Black foam."

Broken Stencil

Allow the stencil to break
let the form shift
there is beauty interwoven in imperfection
discipline in shaving off excess.
When the stencil breaks
we will know.

Freedom pours out like
stories from the mouth of an old musician
who sings from a place only the blues and hues
of jazz are random enough
to reach and retrieve

Like a waterfall that refuses to be dammed!
To be rammed against the floor
to be tamed
to be named anything other than
"Natural life-giver."

Allow the stencil to break.

CHAPTER 4

THE SLAP

The last time my temper got the best of me
I slapped the girl in front of me
she had called me a "fool"
after I refused to cheat in math class.
She retaliated and we got sent to the principal's office
our cheeks stinging from the mutual burn.
While we waited outside near the door
I could see the imprint my hand had left on her face
and knew I had unleashed the gates of hell.

The principal suspended us for two weeks
sentenced us to work in the kitchen
miss classes and tests, and tend to the lawn.
My father drove seven hours
and gave me a fullfront hand slap
like a table tennis champion.
While tears ran down my face
he told me, "You never know what is holding a human life together.
You may be using violence to exert your point
but that person's life may be held together by a thread.
Woe upon thee if ya break it!"

The Vision

I got hit and had a vision
of musicians speaking in tongues
their instruments silent.
The blow came from behind and
the blackout was brief to my recollection—
a ringing sound so loud
I was breakdancing in four weeks.

Common Room Survival

The time came
and all present had to show
their cards on the table
after the town crier had assembled the suspects
in the green house common room.
The truth fell out
like a mudslide of molten lava
and I was captured by the bounty hunter.
Forced to surrender like
every time my heart was broken
or the truth uncovered lust disguised as love.

I drank the magic potion
when the trigger phrase was used: "Is this the boy?"
I was the boy
when the boy was slapped.
Then the boy was slapped again and again.
We had treated the conglomerate like kings
danced to the tune of their music
washed their clothes and filled their buckets with bathing water.
We were asked to go away empty-handed
forced to scrape the bottoms of pots after dinner
for survival.

Packo Flakes

Bucket Packo
formerly referred to as "National Cake"
reminders for those who shaped Afro cuts
in ironing rooms.
The red towel is still drying
held together by a peg.

Harmattan is coming and the wind blows northward.
The kitchen matron has put aside
a snack for the obedient.
Those who were coerced
into selling out their friends to Skete and Chua
for Brownie points have confessed.

We made brew from acidic cashews
plucked from the Botanical Garden in the East
and roasted the nuts behind the brick wall.
The smoke, signals rising into the clouds
sending the message across disputed land
to the eyes of those awake.

Boarding-House Currency

Because we were banned
from carrying money
we deposited a fixed equal amount into the school bank
appointed accounts and wrote cheques to buy supplies like
slippers, buckets and brooms.
But most importantly weekly Shai
our evening refreshments.

Okin biscuit was the currency of my youth
sachets of Lahda powdered milk and tins of Milo
traded like gold bars on the stock market.
The value was real, the crimes real.
Some snorted salt after dinner to have red eyes.
Perfume and contraband were smuggled into the dormitory
through suitcases fixed with false bottoms.
The palms of some teachers
greased by the parents of those who would later rob the bank clean.

Exotic clothes from overseas
like elephant jeans and dungarees
flight and fireman suits
sometimes demanded cartons
while Valentine's cards and teddy bears
were twelve to fifteen packets of biscuits.
There were two kinds of biscuits
the shortcake and the coaster.
The circle and the square, the nourishment to accompany heavy learning
while reading chemistry books like Ababio under fluorescent light.
The main oil reserves were stored in a locker
beside the bench where a guard we called "Baba" slept and kept watch.
Bolted shut with big bulging combination locks
under the care of the "Shai" officer supported
by the "requisition guy"
answering to the House Captain
answering to the Headboy
answering to the Principal
answering to the most high.

Reminders

Who said men don't feel?
I saw a boy get flogged in the ironing room
by a teacher who called the punishment "reminders."
We didn't know what he had done
but the whole school watched
as the lights were shut and we heard
the lashes make contact with skin
now raw from the belt marks
Koboko marks.

When I jacked the prefect's locker
in rebellion against
ill treatment and starvation
I was shamed in front of the girls
made to watch the sun from noon until dinner
my eyes swollen from squinting so long.

My guardian angel had recommended I confess
when the owner of the locker threatened to beat up
a multitude of innocent youth in an attempt to find me
the culprit.

Who said men don't feel?
I was made to watch as all the boys in my year
were beaten and bruised
punished and manhandled
their eardrums ringing like
perforated drum skins.

Betrayal

For how long
have you been played
as the dummy and remained oblivious
to the cantankerous, duplicitous nature of associates
who wore the cloaks of brotherhood?

The Space Between Us

The space between us
was once filled with water
warm from the constant heat
of the blazing summer sun.

The rain started pouring diagonally
naturally, oblique puddles were formed.
We hopscotched between the spaces.
Hurried to find shelter
under the bridge
under the tree
under the bus stop canopy.
Under the rooftop where we lay our heads at night
our hands gripped the handles of
plastic wide white umbrellas
strong enough to withstand
the blowing wind.

Our feet
splashed red, blue, purple and indigo
the rainbow separated the space between us.
Tasted like a silent conversation
between strangers.
The retired trumpet player from across the hall
the bookkeeper who kept an array of exotic birds
and made custom jewellery out of rare stones
and hard cut diamonds
shared tea
and the space between friends
echoed like an endurance trek
a parachute jump
a whitewater raft made from empty petrol barrels
the banging of metal mesh pans with wooden spoons
a memory, reminiscent of our 7:30 salute.

We ate wind from the top of the mountain
broke bread with Roma travellers carrying dusty instruments
composing for a living.
Filling up the decomposing space between us with music.

Together we watched
cold water fall seven hundred feet
the full spectrum of the rainbow
visible to the naked eye.
California sunshine was playing the harp
the space between the strings
tastefully singing like lemongrass and hibiscus
yellow, green and orange.

I am the threshold, the whistleblower
the space between the branches
the space between the stones.
I am a bouquet of red roses shy of my thorns
because they break open the solid cold concrete
into tiny rocks.

The space between the rocks
was once filled with lava
cold from the soft burn
of the shivering winter moon.

We now share space
six feet apart
our eyes communicating
what our lips say behind our masks
our smiles, our frowns, our shopping carts
and drive-through car washes
while the critics howl at the absurdity
of no more social gatherings
The way we once knew them to be.
Where there was actually no space between us
only a beautiful colourful carnival, masquerade parade
marching bands and horn sections.
An ensemble of tambourine players and belly dancers.

We watched the opera in a theatre hall
where the wooden floor was smooth and polished.
The mirrors in the bathroom spotless
like a Dalmatian with imposter syndrome.

The space between the brush and the canvas
the pen and the paper is filled with anticipation and hope.
To insist on a line is to carve an impression
to clothe oneself in costume and camouflage
and embody the script wholeheartedly.

At noon in certain parts of town
we gather in public parks to beat drums
and let the space between us
fill with dancing and laughter.
Circus and drama.
The space between us
was once filled with water.

Bleeding Towel

The towel was red
soaked in an extra-large green plastic bucket
with water fetched from the taps
washed with Ariel, super blue Omo from overseas.
Canoe soap would not do.

It belonged to a boy
who abused his power over those
who had been programmed to bounce to the beat of his drum.
The towel bled red and stained the concrete
where copper wire was used to dry clothes.
At night a young boy would be taken there twice
for wetting the bed.

The next day we saw the burn marks around his neck
initially mistaken for acid from the dreaded skirt and blouse
insects roaming through our blankets at night.
Marks left behind
from an attempted strangulation.
A case of bullying comes to a head
neck-and-neck.

Imprisoned

Blue-collar crimes committed
while Black times spin on the gramophone.
No phone calls
no Nokia phone
no knot 9 knot
no 778
no 265
just prison numbers and solid stone-cold eyes behind bullet-proof glass
palms touching, leaving fingerprints like tribal marks on the surface of the window.
The reckoning
the realization that the brave
are the ones who prayed alone in the temple
who walked silently in the dark.
The bruised and the broken
the burned by fire and iron
the branded
the now lonely flower and the barefoot wanderer
who rang the bell in Notre Dame.

The Legend of Don Shaver

We hear no more distant cries
from the land of sweet potato and Gidigbo
where a sick-bay nurse named Rasheeda
cured the sick boys with her beauty.
Did you know that Don Shaver carved his name into a tree
overlooking the path where lovers' lanes crossed at night?
The scent of Issye Miyake
whispering into classrooms long before his arrival
a story of forbidden love between social classes.
He struck the principal's face in defiance
sent her glasses flying across the dusty road
his power visible in the helicopter blades cutting through the rising smoke
like a butter knife, greased like an agric chicken on Christmas.
To us, he was a bodybuilder glistening orange
underneath the yellow sunflower stalks
revving the engine of a red convertible Mercedes Benz
a living classic
outpacing all of us young bloods.

Redemption

He asked her to reach up and close the louvres
to see her long arms stretch and hold the bars
her fingers are slender, her posture pristine.

Twenty years later, when
he returned looking to marry her sister
she invited him to church, asked him to listen to what
the man had to say.

He didn't remember the words
just the sudden urge to heed the call
to walk up to the altar and submit to a higher power.
He was converted into who he was.

And married his Rachal
instead of Leah.

Habesha

We said
the youth found their voice
with the end of the police brutality movement.

As if
we assumed their voice boxes
had been broken into and we picked the lock
of collective consciousness.

When we knew
our foremothers looked forward to change
and saw a familiar face
reflected in the song harmonized by the branches
of the trees.

As if
we now pour libations
gin, tonic and ancestral waters from Aksum
on Lilies in Valleys where we once shared
stories with drama and laughter.

We sipped
hot jet-black coffee
from tiny cups with no sugar
the smoke clinging to our clothes
watering our eyes and searing memories of a cappella songs
sung in stairways
where tobacco leaves were traded for
earth seeds, whirlwinds and Holy Ghost fire.

Cosmic Rain

The drawing teacher
played guitar in a band on weekends
and the advisor taught us
how to build chairs and cabins beside the lake.
We made strange malleable structures out of kebab sticks
held together by rubber bands and suspended them from the ceiling.

Cosmic dust, Cosmic music, Cosmic rave
raining like electric lights
while papers were due on Tuesday.
The sunflower seed bloomed on the third-floor patio
beside the room where five-foot-
square canvases were rotated ninety degrees
and polished with primary colours.

The body was carved from the buildings
made of basswood, clear glue, copper
and vacuum-sucked plastic
purchased from the store below
leading to the tunnels
where mini-carts roamed in silence
and loud colourful murals
covered the surface of the aging walls.

Solution

Even some plants bloom in desert
where thoughts are constantly plagued
by the scorching, gilded magnificence we have placed
on the concept of martyrdom.

Now, see the blood-sucking informant
disguised as a brother in anguish…
Well, a fox cannot lounge before a lion.
Still, his torture nutures disgust.

Black Bodies

There is a vibe
that draws me to the black sometimes
makes me sit upright
alert
like I know you know I am looking at your uniform, your badge
unabashed
our cousins the Blackfoot like to do things
old-school raw with emotions
speak out in tongues
…mwi choni
say it loud
"Officer! Don't hold my Black body to the floor."

Day in
day out
the day never breaks without the sun coming out to shine.

WE HAVE THE RIGHT TO BE RIGHT

A wise man once noted
Black bodies
were scattered around the world as a direct result of Black bodies
bending
bowing at the cracked feet of a false man, false master, false overseer
breaking skin by cracking whip.

Day in
day out
the day never breaks without the sun coming out to shine.

I have been plotting my escape
my run, my underground railroad return
thinking I'll use education as a shotgun.
Sawed off, cocked back
blow the shackles of misery
clean from our minds.

Hands up, don't shoot.
The scene changes suddenly—
straight out of nowhere
police cars with silent sirens circle the block
blockade the streets.
Licence and registration
licence and obligation
your licence to kill with no fear of repercussions
has me clinging to the powers of melanin.

HANDS UP! DON'T SHOOT!

Day in day out
the day never breaks without
Black bodies being sealed in body bags.
We say
No justice No peace
No verdict No peace
just an empty brown paper bag of excuses
why a Black man can be murdered in his sleep.
I will wash the blood off your sweater
stitch the hole where the bullet entered
and dye it red, black and green.

Day in day out
the day never breaks without the sun coming out to shine.
I see Black bodies lying still on the cold concrete, eyes still
can still feel the fear
still see the silhouettes of the perpetrators
slide free from the blind sword of Justice.
What becomes of the mothers who wail
over promises left unkept
and the futures left behind?

Crossover

In Jos, where we crossed over
from our childhood
where dreams and realities blended into dramas
we beat drums and partook in the endurance trek
played Red Rover
across the dusty field.
Together, we climbed to the summit
of the highest mountain
and surveyed the land
a maximum of five people at the peak.

Who saw the hands
of the soldiers at the tollgate massacre
in Lagos where the people stood up for their rights?
Who gave the order to end the voice of the people
and place us under house arrest

like the rest of the world
in lockdown
during the pandemic?

1968

The immigrant was the called
"The Black Guy" beside "The Desert Girl"
and he chose to become him
to embrace him. To welcome him.
Not to take it as an insult but as an exaltation.
To search the history books
and redefine him
to reassign him to his original post
to sign him to a contract of Black pride with a black pen.
To know him, study him
to see where he was wronged in the past and defend him, defend her.
To wash his wounds with clean water
and soothe him if he cries.
Not to judge him, to guide him
to find him when he is lost.
To encourage him when he is found.

To shadow him
sometimes shadow box ideas of
Black Resistance,
Black Stance, Black Culture,
Black Hair, Black Music, Black Hope.
Black Text written in all caps with Black ink
washed off a wooden protest board with a Black brush
Black allies marching on Black roads chanting
"Black Lives Matter."
Black Love.
Black Family.

What did the athletes do with their Black shoes in 1968?
They walked onto the Black podium with Black socks
for Black poverty with Black beads, Black books
Black leather jackets and Black berets.
All wrapped into a Black glove.
Black fist.
For the bruised and the broken
the burned by fire and iron
the branded, the stranded on the high seas
the sold, the bought
on the rickety Black auction block

the shipped across the Middle Passage
the thrown overboard.
The Black mermaids are showing up on shore
with halos as hashtags and
They demand Justice
They demand Peace.
The reason Number 7 took a knee
during the singing of the American National anthem
as an icon of integrity.

Sankofa

This painting is about
Revolution
Revolution
Revolution.

The transformation from victimization to
"Sankara"
"Sankara"
"Sankara."

Upright, defender of basic human rights.

This is not about 40 acres and a mule.
Reparations.
Reparations.
Reparations.

It is about the eagle's repatriation to that which is already Indigenous to our soul.

SANKOFA.

This painting is about choice
the dichotomy
sometimes appearing as a trifecta of problems.
It is about mental health, breaking down.
About finding oneself asleep in a psych ward.
Sometimes, the inability to choose
in the face of choice
is a choice in itself.
And that choice can drive you mad.

This painting is about family.
About legacy, and the responsibility of carrying one's weight.
About preserving tradition.
Destroying traditions
and reassembling the pieces
like a jigsaw puzzle
depicting an image of the passion of Christ
like a teardrop
from Mary Magdalene's eyes
Mary the mother of JESUS CHRIST.

This painting is about breakdancing,
spray painting, deejaying
and the unpredictable bars of emcees.

It is about the 5th element of hip hop
Knowledge.

Often disregarded.
Highlighted in red.
Illustrated as a human brain connected to three books.
Like the bond between a father, a son and mother as the Holy Ghost.

This painting is about shifting the power structure in colourful ways
by using the sun to shed light
on that which has been kept at bay.
You see, Black matriarchs have risen up
demanding justice for the stolen lives of Michael Brown
Tamir Rice, say her name, Sandra Bland
we've been singing the same song since
Amadou Diallo.

This painting is about beauty
the soft and subtle blue of her skin
the sanctity of melanin.
Queen and Victoria
Queen and Victorious
Amanitore, Amanishakheto
Nubian empress holy reflection of
Black Dionysus.

This painting is about patterns, shapes and lines
the beauty of complexity
the simplicity of an apology
and its adequacy to turn back the hands of time.

Only time will tell.
This time I commit that such a transgression
will Never, Never, Never happen again.

This painting is about Louis Riel
Gabriel Dumont, Big Bear and Poundmaker
uniting to defend what they believed in.

Before he was called crazy
a lunatic on the run
a tyrant deserving of the rope
before the trap doors of gallows swung open
as retribution for spilling the orange blood of Thomas Scott.
We have learned that the power of love is always greater
than the power of war and the rumours of war.

Therefore

this painting is about the movement
call it "SANKOFA"
a reaching back to retrieve what we have forgotten.

It is about Lumumba, Nkrumah, Mandela, Kagame
but most especially
Thomas Sankara and Marcus Garvey.
And the march toward
a future gold-backed Black African currency.

About the Author

KOMI OLAFIMIHAN is a Visual Artist, Futurist and Poet. His performance poetry has, since 2008, reflected a keen sense of musicality and orality, along with a willingness to bend or defy the conventions of the spoken word by integrating live painting and music. He has toured Canada extensively as a performance poet, including notable appearances at Vancouver Island Music Festival, Ottawa VERSeFest, Hillside Community Festival, and Manifesto Festival. He is a former Canadian national slam champion (Canadian Festival of Spoken Word, 2009). His work has been published in *Arc Magazine*, *The Nonprofit Quarterly* (Summer 2022) and *The Great Black North: Contemporary African Canadian Poetry* (Frontenac House, 2013). Komi Olafimihan lives and works in Toronto, Ontario. He operates Studio-olaf 11280597 CANADA INC.

www.komiolaf.com

Write Bloody North publishes groundbreaking voices and legends of spoken word to create innovative, fresh poetry books. A new voice in Canadian publishing, we are an independent imprint of the trail-blazing Write Bloody Publishing (Los Angeles). Beautiful, Canadian-made books.

Want to know more about Write Bloody North books, authors, and events? Join our mailing list at

www.writebloodynorth.ca

WRITE BLOODY NORTH BOOKS

Black Abacus — Ian Keteku
Divine Animal — Brandon Wint
Friends Without Bodies — Brendan McLeod
My Soft Response To The Wars — RC Weslowski
The Problem with Solitaire — Lucia Misch
This Is How We Disappear — Titilope Sonuga
Three Hundred Poems — Komi Olafimihan

www.ingramcontent.com/pod-product-compliance
Lightning Source LLC
Chambersburg PA
CBHW031818110426
42743CB00057B/880